People of the Bible

The Bible through stories and pictures

Joseph and His Brothers

Copyright © in this format Belitha Press Ltd, 1982

Illustrations copyright © Chris Molan 1982

Art Director: Treld Bicknell

First published in the United States of America 1982
by Raintree Publishers, Inc.
205 West Highland Avenue, Milwaukee, Wisconsin 53203
in association with Belitha Press Ltd, London.

Conceived, designed and produced by Belitha Press Ltd.
40 Belitha Villas, London N1 1PD

Moody Press Edition 1983
ISBN: 0-8024-0395-6

First published in Australia in paperback 1982
by Princeton Books Pty Ltd, PO Box 24, Cheltenham, Victoria 53203

ISBN 0 909091 16 1 (Australian)

Printed in Hong Kong by South China Printing Co.

Joseph and His Brothers

RETOLD BY ELLA K. LINDVALL
PICTURES BY CHRIS MOLAN

MOODY PRESS
CHICAGO

There was once an old man called Jacob. He had many children. He had twelve sons and one daughter. Of all his sons, he loved Joseph the best.

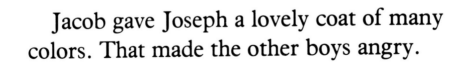

Jacob gave Joseph a lovely coat of many colors. That made the other boys angry.

Then one day, Joseph said to his brothers, "I had a wonderful dream last night. I dreamed that we were all out in the field. We were binding wheat into sheaves. My sheaf stood up, and all your sheaves came and bowed down to it."

The brothers were furious. They said, "Do you think that means you are going to rule over *us*?"

After that, Joseph had another dream. "In this dream the sun and moon and eleven stars bowed down to me," he said.

Now the brothers hated Joseph more than ever.

Some time later, Joseph's brothers were out in the country. They were looking after their father's sheep and goats.

12

Father Jacob said to Joseph, "Go out into the country and find your brothers. Then come back here and tell me how they are getting along."

So Joseph started off.

When the brothers saw Joseph coming across the fields, they said to each other, "Look! Here comes that great dreamer. This is our chance to get rid of him. Let's kill him."

But the oldest brother, Reuben, did not want to kill Joseph. He said, "Don't kill him. Just throw him down into that pit." Reuben thought that later he would come back alone and rescue Joseph.

When Joseph reached his brothers, they took off his coat of many colors. Then they threw him down into the pit. Reuben went away for a while, and the other brothers sat down to eat their lunch.

While they were eating, they looked up and saw some men on camels coming along the road.

The camels were loaded with spices and other things, which the men were going to sell in the land of Egypt.

Then Judah said, "I have an idea! Instead of killing Joseph, why don't we sell him to these traders?"

Quickly they pulled Joseph up out of the pit and sold him to the men for twenty pieces of silver money. Then the traders and their camels and Joseph went on down the road toward far-away Egypt.

After the traders had taken Joseph away, Reuben came back. He looked into the pit. Joseph was not there. Maybe for a moment Reuben thought the other brothers had killed him. He was very upset and said, "What am I going to tell my father?"

The brothers decided what to do. First they killed a goat. Next they put some of the blood on Joseph's coat. Then they took the coat back to their father and said, "We found this coat with blood on it out in the wild lands. It looks like the coat you gave Joseph."

Father Jacob saw that it was Joseph's coat, and he thought that Joseph was dead. He said, "An animal must have eaten him up. I shall never see him again." And Jacob cried.

But Joseph was not dead. Joseph was alive somewhere in the far-off land of Egypt.

Joseph would be in Egypt a long time, far from his home and his father. But God was in Egypt with him. God would take care of Joseph. And someday his father would see him again.

Moody Press, a ministry of the Moody Bible Institute, is designed for education, evangelization, and edification. If we may assist you in knowing more about Christ and the Christian life, please write us without obligation: Moody Press, c/o MLM, Chicago, Illinois 60610.

The Land of the Bible Today

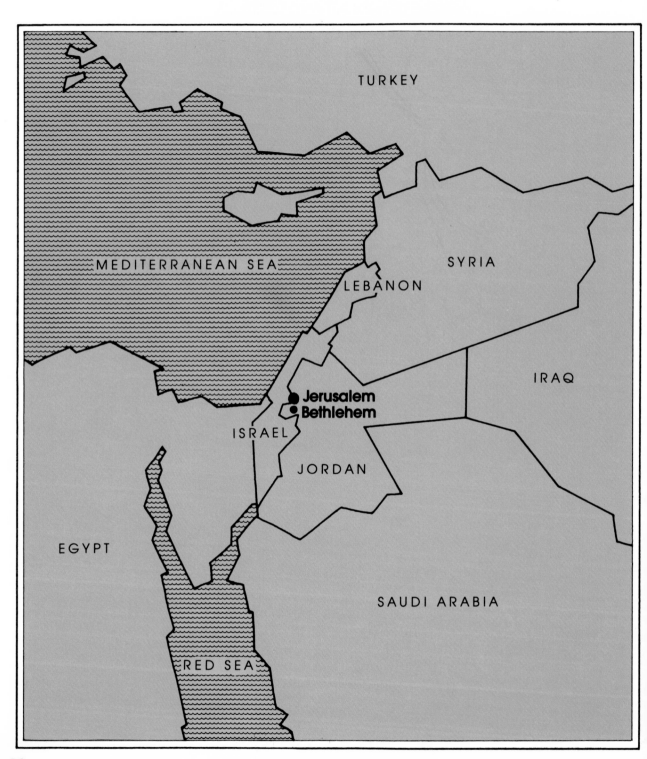